Pigtails and Pigweed

Memoir of My Rural Childhood

Iris Maria Goebel

outskirtspress
DENVER, COLORADO

Pigtails and Pigweed
Memoir of My Rural Childhood
All Rights Reserved.
Copyright © 2014 Iris Maria Goebel
v2.0

Outskirts Press, Inc.
http://www.outskirtspress.com

ISBN: 978-1-4787-2556-5

Outskirts Press and the "OP" logo are trademarks belonging to Outskirts Press, Inc.

PRINTED IN THE UNITED STATES OF AMERICA

This book is lovingly dedicated to my children, who would often ask me what it was like growing up in the "olden days."

Contents

Prelude

"OW! OW! OOOOWWW!!!"

I had scampered up onto the hayrack in our barnyard, and now I couldn't get back down. My mother was pulling me by my arms under the bottom board on the side of the hayrack – and something was hurting badly! After she got me out, she saw that I had been scratched across my stomach by a nail that had been sticking up in the floor of the hayrack where I had been lying.

The above scene is the first memory I have as a young child. It was a warm summer day in 1939, and I was three-and-a-half years old. My Grandmother (my mother's mother) had come to stay with us for a few days on the farm, and we three were walking in the barnyard looking at the different things there. The long scratch that I got on my stomach that day turned into a scar that was still visible many years later.

Beginnings

IF THE REGISTRAR of new births, who came monthly, had been in Rimbey the day that Dad went to register my February 21, 1936, home birth, I would have been officially named "Alexandra Louise von Tettenborn." Dad insisted that his children's names also be recognized as German names. Mom, however, would have preferred giving me shorter Christian names because my last name was already quite long.

Meanwhile, while waiting for the registrar to return, Dad brought home a 50-pound bag of oatmeal, which had *Iris Oats* as the brand name. Mom thought "Iris" was a very nice name and that it would be a much shorter first name for me. So during the next few weeks, she was able to get Dad to accept a change in names. This time, when Dad went to town to register my name one month later, I was given the name "Iris Maria von Tettenborn." (Iris is pronounced "eeris" in the German language.)

I grew up near the end of an era in Central Alberta, Canada, when most farm houses had no electricity, no running water, and no telephones. Most farmers were still using horses to farm their land, and one-room schools were still being used in the rural areas. Within the next decade or so, as the economy began to pick up after World War II, many advantages in country living would begin to take place.

My Family

MY FATHER, BERNHARD von Tettenborn, was born on July 6, 1906, in Tilleda, Prussia, Germany, into a titled family (the nobility) that traces its history back to the mid-1100s. He had a sister, Elisabeth (my Tante Lisa), who was 15 months older, and a sister, Ilse (my Tante Ilse), who was nearly two years younger than he was. Dad's father (my Grossvater), who was twice the age of his wife (my Grossmutter) when they married, died at age 57, leaving his widow to raise their three young children by herself.

As a child, Dad grew up on the same street in Rostock, Germany (near the North Sea), where the famous air ace of the First World War, the Red Baron (Manfred von Richthofen), once lived. Dad immigrated to Canada, when he was 22, with his friend, Wolfgang von Kannenburg, in April 1929, landing at Pier 21 in Halifax, Nova Scotia. Dad and Wolfgang settled in Central Alberta within a few miles of each other. Dad hoped to recoup the family fortune lost in the runaway inflation and depression following World War I, and then return to Germany to live.

My mother, Alma Eritsland, was born on June 19, 1907, in Nassau, Minnesota, USA. Her parents, Anna Marie and Lars Eritsland, who lived in the Bergen area of Norway, were engaged before immigrating to America in 1888 and 1889 respectively; both entered the country through Ellis Island, in Upper New York Bay. They were married in St. Paul, Minnesota, in 1889. Mom was the second youngest in a large family of two boys and eight girls. (The oldest girl died in infancy before the other children were born). Mom's family first lived in Iowa; they then moved to Minnesota before moving across the country to Eugene, Oregon, in 1909. Mom entered Canada with her parents and her four youngest siblings in 1916. They also settled in Central Alberta.

Mom and Dad were married on October 13, 1933. Prior to that, Mom taught for five years at the one-room schoolhouse at Leedale (which is about 15 miles southwest of Rimbey). Dad met Mom in May 1929, when he began working on the Broderson farm, where Mom lived while she was teaching. In the spring of 1931, Dad rented land northeast of Rimbey (in the Springdale area) to farm with his friend, Wolfgang von Kanneburg, who had immigrated to Canada with him. This venture, however, soon turned sour with the land owner, so the rental agreement lasted only one year. The next spring (1932), Dad bought a half section of land (320 acres), which was located about nine miles southwest of Rimbey, from the Canadian Pacific Railroad. He paid six dollars an acre for this land. This is the farm Mom moved to when they were married. Here they settled down to raise their family, becoming the original homesteaders on this raw property that was covered in trees.

My brother, Bernhard (Bernie for short), the first-born in our family, was born on December 18, 1934. He was one year, two months, and three days older than I was – he was my constant playmate when I was growing up.

My oldest sister, Elisabeth Anne (Betty Anne for short) was born on September 6, 1946. (My youngest sister, Linda, and my youngest brother, Mark, were not yet born during the period that this memoir covers; both are mentioned in the Chronology chapter at the end of the book.)

We were poor, but I wasn't aware of this fact because many of our neighbors didn't have much money either during these "dirty thirties," the Great Depression which had become worldwide. Everyone in the community helped their neighbors if there was a need, for example: at harvest threshing time, at firewood sawing bees, when someone's house burned down, when someone was seriously ill, etc.

We had no car during the first 10 years of my childhood; instead, as a family, we rode to town (Rimbey) or to neighbors' places in a wagon or a buggy pulled by a team of two horses. During the winter months, we rode in a cutter (a light sleigh) that was pulled by one or two horses. We covered our legs with blankets and put our feet on the warmed-in-the-oven stones that were tucked inside the straw that was placed on the floor of the cutter. When we went to town, we tied our horses to the hitching rails that were built along a side street for that purpose. Rimbey also had a livery stable (small barn), where people could pay to tie their horses – here they could eat hay and be sheltered. We never used the livery stable.

Sometimes Dad or Mom rode a saddle horse if they needed to go somewhere. Bernie and I rode our horses when we attended school. Bernie's horse (a light dappled gray color) was called Bluebell, and my horse (a reddish bay color) was called Babe. We rode bareback. If the weather was pleasant, we would sometimes walk a mile or two to play with friends for the afternoon.

Mom's youngest sister, Esther, and her family lived on a farm about seven or eight miles northwest of us. In the summer, Mom and Dad would sometimes drive with Bernie and me in the buggy to see them; this short distance away allowed us to get home in time to do the evening chores and milk the cows. However, when I was eight years old, Aunt Esther and her family moved far away (near Jasper, Alberta) so we couldn't visit them anymore.

We didn't drive with horses to visit any other relatives because they lived too far away. During those years, however, Mom's mother (my Grandma) and some of Mom's siblings, who had cars, drove to our home to see us. My first visit to see Grandma and Mom's brother, Paul, who lived about 30 miles away on a farm at Leslieville (near Rocky Mountain House), was at Easter in 1946; we had recently bought our new truck and could now easily make the trip there and back home again in one day.

Our parents both came from Lutheran backgrounds; however, there was no Lutheran church in the area where we were living. Bernie and I were baptized by our Uncle Andrew Hjortaas (who was a Lutheran pastor, married to Mom's older sister, Emma) when they came to visit us in the summer of 1939.

Mom told us Bible stories when we were young; later, when we could read, our parents gave us *Egermeiers' Bible Story Book* so we could read these stories ourselves.

Dad taught us to pray this German table prayer when we were little:

> *Komm, Herr Jesu; sei du unser Gast;*
> *Und segne, was du uns bescheret hast.*

The English translation of this common table prayer is:

> Come, Lord Jesus, be our Guest;
> And let these gifts to us be blessed.

We also learned to pray this German nighttime prayer when we went to sleep:

> Ich bin klein,
> Mein herz ist rein,
> Soll niemand drin wohnen
> Als Jesus alien.

English Translation:

> I am small,
> My heart is pure,
> No one shall live in it
> But Jesus alone.

We children grew up bi-lingual: we spoke German with Dad and English with Mom and with each other. Dad taught us to read and write German, using the old German script. After Bernie and I started public school, Dad requested that we each write 15 lines every day in German about any subject; he would correct our writing at the end of the day.

Mom spoke and wrote Norwegian, but she thought it would be too much for us to learn three languages at the same time, so we never did learn Norwegian. Mom learned the German language from Dad's speaking German with us. She always read the letters that Dad's relatives sent from Germany, but she was fearful of mispronouncing the words, so she never carried on a German conversation. In later years, if Dad had momentarily forgotten the German word for something, he would ask Mom what it was, and she would always know it.

Our Farmhouse

DAD BUILT A small, two-room house before he was married; it had a combined kitchen-living room and a bedroom. Before I was born, Mom and Dad built a lean-to kitchen on the north side of the house, which gave us considerably more room.

Below is a brief description of our three-room farmhouse.

The entrance door into the kitchen from outside was located on the east side of the house. To the right of the door, when you entered, stood a large wood-burning cooking range against the east wall; cupboards with a counter between them (that had a box for firewood underneath) were attached to the north wall; and a small eating table, which had a pull-out bench at the back, where Bernie and I sat when we ate our meals, was along the west wall. An overhead china cabinet was attached to the wall above the table. A closet for hanging outdoor coats (that hid behind the connecting door between the kitchen and living room when it was closed) was built beside the eating table on the west wall. To the left of the door that opened into the living room on the south wall was a washstand that held a basin (where we washed up) and a water pail with a dipper (from which we drank), and in the southeast corner of the kitchen, to the left of the outside entrance door, was a stand that held our hand-turned cream separator.

When you entered the living room from the kitchen, to the right were a treadle sewing machine and a bookcase along the north wall. Another bookcase and an upright piano stood against the west wall, and a battery-run radio sat on a small table in the southwest corner. A cot for sitting and sleeping on was placed along the south wall. The front door was built near the southeast corner of the living room. A small wood-burning heater stood beside the east wall around the corner from the front door. To the left of the heater on the east wall was a doorway, which went into the bedroom; and in the northeast corner of the living room, beside the bedroom doorway, sat a covered wood box that held firewood. A rocking chair and a few extra chairs were placed around the room.

The small bedroom was on the east end of the house, and was entered through the curtained doorway that was cut in the wall between the wood box and the heater in the living room. This room held a double bed that fit snugly along the south wall and also touched the west and east walls of the bedroom; a dresser-type stand stood under the east-facing window; and a large clothes closet with shelving (all hiding behind a large curtain) was built along the entire north wall.

When we were small, Bernie and I slept in twin-size trundle beds (with wheels) that were stored under our parents' bed during the daytime; at night, these beds were rolled out into the middle of the living room where we slept. The mattresses were refilled with fresh straw every now and then to keep them firm. When we outgrew the trundle beds, Bernie slept in the attic on a mattress placed on the unfinished floor. To get to his bed at night, he would go outside with a lantern and climb a ladder to reach the outside door of the attic, and then go inside. I slept on the cot in the living room.

In the summer, when we had overnight visitors, Bernie and I slept in the barn hayloft, where we would fall asleep listening to the mysterious sounds of mice rustling in the hay. In the fresh, early morning, we would wake to the gentle sound of pigeons cooing in the rafters.

The house had no bathroom, so we used an outhouse that sat among the trees some distance from the house. At nighttime, when we were young, we used a chamber pot that stood under the bed when we had to "go." Mom bathed us in front of the warm kitchen stove in a large galvanized washtub. When we were older, we gave ourselves sponge baths in privacy.

The house was not insulated. During the winter months, Bernie and I wore long underwear, long stockings, and sweaters inside the house to keep warm. In the cold mornings, we often had fun sliding our tongues over Jack Frost's icy creations that formed on the single-pane windows inside the house.

There was a time when our house became infested with bedbugs. Ugh! To get rid of these disgusting pests, Mom fumigated the house in the summer with a compound that smelled like sulfur. Meanwhile, we all camped out for three days in a granary near the pig pen. We could hear the pigs squealing and grunting *oink-oink-oink* as they rooted around in the dirt or chomped down on a meal of chop (ground-up grain) that we fed them. Thankfully, the fumigation took care of the bedbugs.

In 1943, Mom and Dad began to build an addition to our house, so we would have more room. Downstairs were a large living room and a large bedroom for our parents, and upstairs were two bedrooms, one for Bernie and one for me. Over the next five years, Mom and Dad continued working on this building project, as time permitted. Bernie and I moved into our new bedrooms when they were finished in the spring of 1948 – we had to climb a ladder to reach them until the stairway going upstairs was built. Mom and Dad completely finished the interior of this new addition before they cut a doorway through the wall that joined the old house with the new part in the late summer of 1948. Now our house seemed HUGE!

Life on the Farm

MY PARENTS WERE busy with "mixed farming," as were most farmers in Canada during the middle of the 1900s. This meant that besides planting and harvesting various crops, they also had many animals that were used on the farm to help provide food and money for the family. Most farmers could still make a living off their land, so there was no need to seek outside employment to help supplement their income.

Dad had bought a half section of land (320 acres) from the Canadian Pacific Railroad in the spring of 1932. This farm was raw land covered in trees; no one had lived there before. Some of the first major things that had to be done were: dig a well for water, build a house and barnyard buildings, clear the land so that crops could be planted, and build fences around the property so that the animals couldn't wander away. This is where Mom and Dad settled down to live and raise a family after their wedding on October 13, 1933.

In 1943, after much hard work and thrift during the Depression years, Mom and Dad were able to pay off the mortgage on this half-section of land. The next year (1944), they bought a quarter section of cleared land (160 acres) that was one-and-a-half miles north of our home place. (In 1951, they bought the quarter section that was immediately north of our home place. This property was also cleared of trees. My parents now farmed a section of land - 640 acres.) All of our Alberta farmland was located in what is called the "parkland" (treed) area, not the "prairie," which was in the southern part of the province.

Life was busy and hard during those early years because there were still no modern conveniences on the farm. We had no car or truck, no tractor, no electricity, no running water, no telephone. Farming was done with horses, cows were milked by hand, water had to be hand pumped to fill the water trough in the barnyard for the animals to drink, and water had to be carried in pails to the house for drinking, cooking, bathing, washing clothes, etc. (Later, a gas motor was installed to pump water from the well.)

In the early years, Mom made her own soap out of rendered pig fat and lye for washing the clothes. I don't know her soap-making process; I just remember watching her cut the finished soap into bars after it had cooled and hardened in the pans into which she had poured it.

To wash our dirty laundry in those first years, Mom scrubbed the clothes on a wooden washboard that stood inside a large galvanized washtub that was filled with warm water. She squeezed the dirty water out of the clothes by hand and then rinsed the clothes in the washtub that was now filled with clean water. She then had to wring the water out of the clothes again by hand before she could hang them on the outdoor clothesline to dry. In the winter, the clothes would freeze stiff in a matter of minutes!

In the early 1940s, Mom used a washing machine with a hand wringer, where an attached wooden handle, pulled back and forth by hand, moved the clothes around in the water. The wet clothes then had to be individually and carefully put through the hand-turned wringer to squeeze out the dirty water. The dirty water then had to be drained off into pails and emptied outdoors. The machine was again filled with clean water to hand-agitate and rinse the clothes. The clothes had to be put through the hand wringer a second time to squeeze out all the excess water before they could be hung on the line to dry.

After World War II, a gas-powered washing machine with an automatic wringer was purchased. Even though the washing machine still had to be hand-filled with water and then drained off, as before, laundry day was now much easier.

With all these different clothes-washing methods, water had to be hauled in pails to the house, heated in big boilers (tall metal containers) on the kitchen stove, and then poured into the washtub or the washing machine. Special white clothes, such as tablecloths, tea towels, and dress shirts, were "cooked" in boiling water on the kitchen stove for about 15 minutes to remove the stains and to keep them white. A bluing liquid was also added to the rinse water to help whiten the clothes. Laundry washing was very time consuming!

(Mom and Dad never had an automatic washer because running water was never installed in the house. In later years, when a Laundromat was built in Rimbey, Mom took the laundry there.)

To iron the clothes, they first had to be sprinkled with water and rolled up in a large towel to keep them moist. Once the clothes were damp throughout, we ironed them with "sad irons." (A sad iron is a smoothing iron that is solid and flat, and pointed at both ends.) The sad irons were heated on the kitchen stove. A wooden removable handle was clamped onto the top of a sad iron, which was then used for ironing. When the sad iron began to cool off, it was returned to the stove to be reheated; the wooden handle was then clamped onto another hot sad iron so that one could continue ironing. Mom had three sad irons.

At night, we lit several coal oil lamps that burned kerosene for fuel and placed them in different rooms for lighting. (Coal oil is another name for kerosene.) Kerosene was poured into the bottom of the lamp, which was usually made of glass so one could see how much fuel was left. At the center of the lamp sat a metal base that held a wick, which dipped down into the kerosene, and a small turning wheel for adjusting the flame. The wick was lit with a match, and after the glass chimney was set down on the metal base, the wick was re-adjusted for a better flame. Periodically, the wick needed to be trimmed, and the chimney needed to be cleaned because it would blacken if the flame flared up too high. To turn off the lamp, you simply cupped your hand behind the top of the chimney and blew out the flame.

We used outdoor lanterns, which also burned kerosene, when we milked the cows in the barn or if we had to go outside at night.

The first barn Dad built in the farmyard was a log building that had a straw roof. There were fenced-in enclosures built on both sides of the barn that held the hay and straw that Dad stacked there to use for caring for the animals that were housed inside the barn. Some of the horses, cows, and sows with their litters of newborn pigs used this barn. Later, when the "horse" barn was built, this log barn was used mainly for milking; that's why we called it the "cow" barn.

The much larger horse barn was completed in 1939. The first level was built of logs, and the large hayloft on top was built of lumber. Later, we milked the cows in this barn, but we always still called it the "horse" barn.

Dad had painted the year 1939 in Roman numerals – MCMXXXIX – on the south gable side of the barn. This paint must have faded because, when I was six or seven, I remember Dad being up on a ladder repainting the numerals in bright red; Mom was steadying the ladder, and Bernie and I were standing around watching.

Some of my daily chores were: wash and/or dry dishes, help tidy the rooms, some baking as I got older, daily wash the cream separator bowl and its different parts, gather eggs, bring the cows home from their pasture for milking, help milk the cows, feed milk to the calves, chop and bring in wood to the kitchen and living room wood boxes, and bring the horses home from their pasture when Dad needed them to work on the farm. The north pasture was for cows, and the south pasture was for horses – both pastures were heavily wooded and extended one mile from west to east across our two home quarters. I usually rode my horse to find the cows and horses and then bring them home. Fortunately a few of the cows and the horses had bells tied around their necks so I could hear them when I got closer to them.

Mail on our rural postal route was delivered on Tuesdays and Saturdays. Our metal mailbox was set up beside the main road that was three-quarters of a mile north of our house. To pick up our mail, I would either walk that distance or ride my horse. The main telephone line to Rimbey went past the corner by our mailbox, and I remember being fascinated by the "humming" sound the telephone wires made when the wind was blowing.

The Eaton's catalogue was a staple in nearly every Canadian household. This was a mail-order catalogue published by Eaton's, a major Canadian retail store from 1884 to 1976. The catalogue sold such products as clothing, pharmaceuticals, books, furniture, china, farm tools, etc. Pre-fabricated houses were at one time sold through the Eaton's catalogue; however, by the time I was growing up these were no longer featured.

In the early years on the farm, Mom ordered most of our clothing, fabric for sewing, and gifts from the Eaton's catalogue. Bernie and I were always excited when the Eaton's winter catalogue arrived in our mailbox because it displayed several additional pages of Christmas toys. Some of these we put on our wish list!

I fractured my left collarbone when I was seven. One morning, Bernie and I went with Dad when he drove a team of horses out to the back field with the stoneboat so he could haul rocks off the plowed field. The stoneboat, a flat platform that skidded over the ground on log runners, had gaps between the boards that formed the platform; the boards were nailed to the runners. Every time Dad drove the horses forward to pick up more rocks, Bernie and I ran behind, laughing, as we jumped on and off the stoneboat. Suddenly, I flipped through a gap between the boards and was dragged along the ground several feet before Bernie realized what had happened and shouted to Dad to stop the horses. Dad laid me on the grass at the edge of the field, wrapped up in his jacket, and continued gathering more stones until it was time to drive back to the barnyard for lunch. I could move both of my arms so they weren't broken, but my upper left arm continued to hurt. Mom suspected that I had fractured my collarbone and thought I should probably see the doctor in town. However, I was terrified of going to the doctor, having never been to one, so we never went. Instead, Mom wrapped my arm in a sling over my shoulder, which I wore for many days. This helped ease the pain, and eventually the pain went away entirely. The small bump (caused by the fracture) that formed on the top of my collarbone, finally disappeared when I was in my early teens.

Our Horses

WHEN I WAS growing up, we always had several horses on our farm. In the early years of my parents' marriage, horses were essential for carrying out all the different farm operations, such as pulling machinery, hauling hay, threshing, grinding grain to feed the animals, etc. They were also used for travelling and for riding to school.

These are the horses that Mom and Dad had on our farm while I was growing up:

<u>Nellie</u> - brown color, work horse

<u>Peter</u> - dark gray color, work horse

<u>Dolly</u> – white color, work horse

<u>Star</u> – white color, work horse - parents were Dolly and Peter

<u>Pat</u> – brown color, work horse - parents were Dolly and Peter

Pearl – brown color, work horse - parents were Nellie and Peter

<u>Fay</u> - reddish bay color, part thoroughbred – was Dad's saddle horse, but also used as a work horse when needed

<u>Fairy</u> - reddish sorrel color, a slightly larger part-thoroughbred horse, also used as a work horse when needed – Mom's rode her to Benjamin School while she was teaching when the roads were extremely muddy

<u>Bluebell</u> - light dappled-gray color - Bernie's school horse – ridden without a saddle

<u>Babe</u> - reddish bay color - my school horse - also ridden without a saddle

<u>Tuck</u> - reddish bay color - part thoroughbred - not used for field work - was older when bought for the purpose of raising a colt from her (unfortunately, the colt was born stillborn)

<u>Tiny</u> – dark brown color – was deaf – was a pony for Bernie and me to ride on when we were small – I rode her by myself when I was four years old

There was an incident that involved Tuck. When Mom was teaching at Benjamin School, Tuck pulled the cutter that we rode in to get to school during the winter months. Dad had built the cutter tongue in such a way that allowed Tuck to run in the right track on the road, instead of running in the deep snow in the middle of both tracks. One very cold and blustery day, when it was time to leave for home after school was let out, Mom brought Tuck out of the school barn, where she had been tied during the day, and hitched her to the cutter. Somehow, on this day, Mom hadn't properly placed the bridle bit in Tuck's mouth so she could be steered when being driven. (The bridle had been removed in the morning so Tuck could eat the hay in the manger.). As we drove through the schoolyard gate to get to the road, Mom suddenly discovered she couldn't control Tuck. And like all horses at the end of the day, Tuck was in a hurry to get home. She rounded the corner out of the schoolyard too sharply, causing the cutter to hit the right gate post. *Smack!* The cutter broke apart, and Tuck took off running for home.

There was never much traffic going past our country school, so it now looked like Mom, Bernie, and I would have to walk home - nearly four miles. Fortunately, however, soon after our cutter accident happened, our neighbor, Nels Mogensen, drove past the schoolyard with a team of horses pulling a sleigh. He took us to his house, which left us only a mile-and-a-half from our place. When Tuck arrived home with some of the broken pieces of the cutter trailing behind her, Dad guessed what had happened and came looking for us. It was almost dark outside when he found us at the Mogensen place and brought us home. It had been a very long day.

Our Cows

IN THEIR EARLY years, Mom and Dad raised a mixture of cows, which they milked twice a day, morning and evening. Some of the calves and cows were sold to add to their income as needed. However, not much money was made selling non-purebred cows – during the Depression years, one of their mature cows sold for only $13! So in 1940, they began raising registered purebred Red Poll cattle, a breed known to be good milkers and good for beef. Mom and Dad eventually maintained a herd of about 30-35 Red Polls. The heifers were kept on the farm to become future milkers, and the bull calves were sold to other Red Poll breeders. The bull calves claimed a good price when sold, making this a good source of income on the farm.

At first, when Mom and Dad started with Red Polls, they kept one large Holstein cow from their previous mix because she was an excellent milker. One spring day, during calving season, Bernie and I were watching her give birth in the barnyard. Suddenly, to our great surprise, we noticed another calf was being born! Twins! That was the only time this occurred while I was growing up.

When Bernie was nine years old, Dad said he was old enough now to start milking some of the cows. Not to be outdone, I said I wanted to start milking too! I was eight years old. At first, we each milked a couple of cows in the old cow barn, which was a small log building, while Dad milked the rest. During the winter months, when all the barn doors and windows were closed, a cosy feeling developed as we milked by lantern light. The surrounding smells of cows and hay in the mangers all added to the ambiance. Dad taught us to sing German songs while we were milking so it wouldn't seem such a chore. Some of the songs we sang were: *O Tannenbaum; Du, Du, Liegst Mir im Herzen; Lustig ist das Zigeunerleben; Muss I' Denn.*

Later on, we did the milking in the new horse barn. In time, as we became better milkers, Mom and Dad paid us for milking, so much per pound. This was a good incentive to get us to strip all the milk out of the cow. After milking each cow, we weighed the milk, and then recorded this amount on a piece of paper that was tacked to the inside of the barn door. At the end of the month, we were paid for our milking - this usually amounted to about $3.50 each, sometimes more, sometimes less. Now that we were "rolling in money," we each opened up a bank account in the Bank of Montreal in town.

Each day, we set aside one or two quarts of the raw fresh milk for our family's use. The rest of the milk was poured into a hand-turned cream separator, which separated the cream from the whole milk. The separator had two pouring spouts: cream came out one spout, and skim milk came out the other.

Some of this skim milk was fed in pails to the weaned calves in their pen; the rest of the skim milk was poured into the troughs for the pigs to drink.

The cream was stored in a large, metal cream can. To keep the cream fresh and cold, they attached a rope from the cream can to the top of a dug well, which was near the barnyard, and then lowered the cream can into the water. When the cream can was full, the cream was sold at the Rimbey creamery. They used the money they were paid for the cream to buy groceries in town.

At first, Mom and Dad used some of their cream to church their own butter at home. I remember making butter by shaking cream in a quart jar for several minutes until clumps of butter separated from the buttermilk. The buttermilk was poured off into a pitcher to use later. The butter was squeezed to remove the remaining buttermilk, and then seasoned with a bit of salt to make it tasty. After World War II, when money wasn't quite as "tight," Mom and Dad bought butter ready-made at the creamery because it cost only two cents more per pound than what they were paid per pound for their cream.

Beginning around 1947, the Alberta government required milk inspectors to visit (on a monthly basis) all the farms that raised registered purebred cattle so that each cow would have her milk tested. The milk inspector tested the milk in the evening, stayed overnight, and then tested the milk again in the morning before going to the next farm.

When we were in grade eight, Dad gave Bernie and me each a heifer so we could earn some money for ourselves when they eventually had calves. The agreed-upon deal was that Dad would get half of the money when the calf was sold (for the cost of feed and care), and we would get the other half.

Unfortunately, my heifer died in a freak accident before she had a calf. One day, when she didn't come home from the cow pasture with the rest of the herd, Dad and Bernie went searching for her. They found her – dead – among the trees in the pasture. She had caught the end of her tail in the barbed wire fence and pulled the brush part off her tail as she struggled to get free and had bled to death.

Bernie didn't fare any better with his heifer. She wouldn't conceive, even after several monthly attempts – so she was shipped off to market.

That was the end of our livestock venture.

Our Other Animals

BESIDES HORSES AND cows, Mom and Dad raised other animals for the purpose of putting food on the table or adding to their farm income. Here are the additional animals that we had on the farm while I was growing up.

PIGS

There were always pigs on the farm when I was growing up – one large mature boar, several mother sows often with litters of piglets, and many midsize young pigs being raised to ship to market for butchering. The pigs were kept in a large, fenced-in pasture (of a few acres) south of the barnyard. A creek ran through the pig pasture near the barnyard fence, where the pigs often wallowed in the water and rooted around in the mud. A large straw-covered shed for shelter was built on the other side of the creek at the edge of the pigpen.

The pigs were fed chop (ground up grain) and the

leftover skim milk twice a day. As soon as the pigs heard the granary door slam open when we entered to scoop up the chop, they knew it was feeding time. They would crowd around the pigpen fence by the granary, setting off a loud squealing racket. The chop and milk were poured into several wooden troughs, where the pigs would then jockey around to get the best position so they could greedily and noisily slurp up the food.

I vaguely remember seeing Mom and Dad butcher a big pig when I was little. The dead pig was hung on a high crossbeam, where it was gutted. Mom and Dad had obviously butchered several pigs before because they had built a small, walk-in "smoke" shed near our house, where they hung the ham shanks above a small fire to be cured in the smoke that wafted upward. I also remember watching my parents make blood sausage and jellied head cheese meat.

Most of our pigs were sold for butchering at the slaughterhouse. We didn't have a scale to weigh the pigs, so Dad used a piece of twine that had a knot tied on it at a certain length. He held this string around the pig, just behind its front legs. If the end of the string and the knot came together, he knew the pig was the right weight to be shipped to market.

Until we had our own truck, Dad hired a neighbour with a truck to take our pigs to market in town. I enjoyed watching the pigs as they were poked and prodded to get them to walk up the pig chute into the truck box. After we bought our own truck in 1946, Dad took the pigs to market by himself.

Some days in the spring, when the pigpen creek had overflowed its banks from all the melting snow, Bernie and I would skate on the ice that had formed overnight on the pasture grass. One morning, when we were skating, the angry boar suddenly appeared and began to chase after Bernie. I was standing on the far side of the ice patch, watching in horror, as the boar got closer and closer to Bernie. I could only imagine the gruesome scene that would take place once he caught up with Bernie. Thankfully, our dog, Bobby, saved the day! (You will read about him later.) Bobby, quick as a flash, raced across the pigpen and caught the back leg of the boar, causing him to spin around and then charge after Bobby. This allowed Bernie to escape to safety. A catastrophe was averted!

SHEEP

When I was five years old, Mom and Dad decided to try their hand at raising sheep, with the hope that this venture would prove to be another good source of income. In the fall, they purchased a small flock of several female sheep and a ram from a neighbour.

The sheep were kept and fed in a pen that was attached to the southeast side of the barnyard. For shelter during the winter, they could enter a small shed that had a straw roof.

The sheep were all fat and woolly and seemed quite tame. One day, while Mom and Dad were tending to the sheep, Bernie and I took turns sitting on the ram. Bernie's ride went very well, but my experience wasn't so pleasant. When I jumped off the ram and was walking toward the edge of the pen to leave, the ram suddenly came up behind and bowled me over, butting me with his head. *Ouch!* I burst into tears and quickly scampered over the fence. After that, I had a healthy respect for the ram and never got close to him again.

Unfortunately, this sheep experience didn't turn out well. Several of the lambs died the next spring, and there may have been other reasons too. Anyway, Mom and Dad decided to sell the whole herd.

CHICKENS

Mom and Dad always raised dual-purpose poultry: Barred Rocks and Rhode Island Reds, which were good for meat and eggs. Dad built a good-sized chicken shed that stood near the southwest corner of our barnyard. Inside, at the back, several long poles, built about four feet off the floor, reached across from one side of the shed to the other side - here the chickens would roost at night. At the other end, to the immediate left of the door where we entered, were several tiers of nest-like boxes, where the hens laid their eggs. At the bottom of the large door was a small door where the chickens could go in and out during the daytime. Hawks and weasels were the usual predators - hawks during the day and weasels at night. We always needed to remember to shut the little chicken door each evening so that weasels couldn't get in and catch some of the chickens.

There were always several roosters in the flock, so the eggs were fertile. To raise more chickens during the early years on the farm, in the spring, Mom would set about a dozen eggs under each of the "broody" hens (those that began to "*cluck cluck cluck*" and wanted to stay in the egg-laying boxes) so they could begin incubating the eggs. Twenty one days later new baby chicks would hatch. The mother hens took care of raising their own chicks, guiding and guarding them as they roamed all over the barnyard, scratching around for grain and insects to eat.

During later years, Mom bought day-old chicks and raised them inside a warm, low-lying shelter she built near our farmhouse, where she was able to keep a close eye on them. Here the chicks lived with plenty of food and water until they were big enough to fend for themselves out in the barnyard.

We always enjoyed our fried chicken dinners!

GEESE

During the first years on the farm, Mom tried to raise some geese with their goslings. They would spend a lot of time nibbling on the grass around the creek in the pigpen and splashing and swimming in the water. However, there were always several coyotes living and hunting in the woods and fields nearby, and they eventually caught most of the geese. This was quite discouraging, so after a few years, Mom gave up trying to raise them.

I have only a vague memory of seeing geese around the barnyard - and the huge goose eggs used for baking! I must have been quite young at the time.

TURKEYS

I also have a faint memory of seeing a large turkey tom proudly strutting and shuffling around in our barnyard, with all his long tail feathers grandly fanned out in a half circle behind him. Did the coyotes do away with the turkeys too?

DOGS

The first dog that I recall living on our farm was called Zenta. She was a mid-size dog and had long hair that was tannish-gray in color. Zenta didn't stay around long when I was little because she soon decided to live at the Cummimgs house, our neighbors who lived about a mile away "as the crow flies" (meaning kitty-corner through the woods).

The dog I grew up with was called Bobby. He may have been one of Zenta's puppies, but I am not certain. He was born with a short, bobbed tail, so we named him "Bobby." He arrived at our place when he was an adorable little bundle of fur, mostly black in color, with highlights of brown and yellow throughout.

Bobby grew up to be a big, shaggy-haired dog. Not only was he a big help with bringing the cows home from the pasture at milking time, he was also a great playmate for Bernie and me.

Bobby would occasionally disappear from the farm, most likely to visit other dogs that lived in the neighborhood. On one particular spring morning, when Bernie and I were riding to school, Bobby had been missing for a number of days. We were travelling on the unfinished road that headed south toward the Mogensen corner, when suddenly our horses shied at something they saw moving in the trees on the west side of the road. Both horses lurched to their left, causing Bernie and me to fall off on the right. We discovered it was Bobby, coming home through the trees, who had caused our horses to jump aside! I came close to losing the sight in my right eye that morning; a branch that lay on the ground where I fell punctured my eye socket in the corner just above my eyeball.

CATS

We had a variety of cats on the farm when I was small. They were a big help in controlling the mouse population in the barns and other out buildings. One summer, when I was eight years old, our Cummings neighbors gave us two little fluffy kittens: an orange tabby for Bernie and a dusty "pink" (my word at the time) kitten for me. How we loved them! Sadly, one morning when I opened our kitchen screen door, I found my kitten lying dead on the doorstep. Was it sick? Was it killed by a rival tomcat in the area? Needless to say, I was heartbroken by this loss.

Later, all the cats on our farm died – feline distemper was suspected. Unfortunately, this highly infectious disease hung around our farm for a number of years because any new cats or kittens we brought to our place would soon die.

Mom on load of hay, with Bernie and Iris 1937

Iris and Bernie with a calf 1938

Bernie and Iris sitting on Peter 1938

Iris on the swing with cat and Bernie 1938

Iris and Bernie reading a book 1938

Iris and Bernie sitting on a horse 1939

Iris and Bernie riding Tiny, south of horse barn 1940

Iris and Bernie 1940

Bernie, Iris sitting on the ram 1941

Our house 1942

Planting and Harvesting

MOM AND DAD "lived off the land" as much as possible during the Depression years. They grew their basic needs in order to feed their family and their animals. Anything extra was sold or bartered to provide an income so they could buy the things the farm didn't produce, e.g. sugar, salt, tools, farm equipment, etc. They also saved money so they could pay off the land they had purchased. Below are some of the major farm activities that provided food and farm income.

GARDENING

Mom always planted a huge garden in the spring so we would have plenty of vegetables to eat during the winter months. When Bernie and I were older, we helped with the weeding and hoeing, and with thinning out the plants in the rows so they wouldn't be so crowded. We enjoyed eating the different fresh vegetables, both raw and cooked, as they came into season. I helped Mom pick beans and peas to prepare them for canning. We also grew asparagus, which we enjoyed eating as soon as the new spears were big enough to harvest in the spring. Our rhubarb was made into tasty pies, and Mom also canned rhubarb for later use.

In the fall, the remaining garden vegetables were dug up and stored in the cool root cellar to use during the winter months. A root cellar is a large hole dug into the ground that is large enough to stand up and walk around in. The roof, covered in sod or some other material, is held in place by several wooden support beams. The root cellar has an entrance door, with steps going down into the interior.

At first, Mom and Dad built a root cellar in the front yard between the house and the cow barn, where they stored the canning and all the fresh garden vegetables that they had harvested. I remember, as a small child, walking down the root cellar steps into the dank interior with Mom, holding a lantern in her hand so she could see the vegetables that she needed to get.

Later, so they could have their stored food close at hand, Mom and Dad cut out a piece of the kitchen floor (approximately 30 inches square) and dug a root cellar underneath. The cut-out floor piece, with hinges attached on one side, was then placed securely over the root cellar opening. It was then raised like a trap door whenever someone needed to climb down the ladder to bring something up from the root cellar.

Root vegetables, such as potatoes, carrots, beets, and turnips were tucked inside large wooden bins that were filled with soil and sand. The filled canning jars were stored on shelves that were built above the bins. During the coldest part of winter, a slow-burning lantern was hung in the root cellar so that nothing would freeze.

BERRY PICKING

In the late summer, Mom would buy cases of peaches and pears, which she then canned in quart jars so we would have fruit to eat during the next several months. We didn't have any fruit trees on the farm because the growing season was not long enough for the fruit to mature.

The strawberries and raspberries that grew in the garden north of our house were enjoyed fresh with cream and sugar; some were made into jam to enjoy on warm toast or fresh-baked biscuits.

We also picked (1) Saskatoon berries that grew on bushes and small trees beside the ditches by the roads, (2) high-bush cranberries that grew in our back cow pasture, and (3) blueberries that grew in our neighbors' vacant pasture across the road. We served the fresh blueberries with cream and sugar. We also enjoyed eating some of the fresh Saskatoon berries with cream and sugar, but most of the Saskatoon berries were canned in quart jars to be eaten later. Mom turned the cranberries into jelly.

HAYING

Dad grew several fields of hay (timothy, alfalfa, red clover, sweet clover) to feed to the horses and cows during the winter months. The summer haying season was always busy. When the hay was ready, Dad cut it with a hay mower that was pulled by a team horses. After the cut hay had dried in the field for a couple of days (longer if it rained and got wet), he would use a hay rake, which was also pulled by a team of horses, to turn the hay over into rows so it would dry out completely.

When the rows of hay were dry, the hay was loaded with pitchforks onto the hayrack, which was pulled by a team of horses. The horses then pulled the full load of hay over to where a haystack was being built out on the field; here the hay was unloaded (again by pitchfork), and then someone on top of the haystack would re-position the hay around so that a solid haystack was built. The top of the haystack was then rounded so rain would run off. Many hayrack loads of hay had to be hauled to complete just one haystack. If it was a large field, several haystacks were built out on the field. Some loads of hay were also brought into the barnyard and pitchforked up into the barn hayloft. Mom helped Dad with this work when Bernie and I were too small to help.

When Bernie was older, he helped to mow and rake the hay. I was 10 years old when I first drove the team of horses forward to raise the "stacker" that threw the hay up on top of the haystack, where Dad stood to re-position the hay. After the hay had been dislodged from the stacker, I then had to back up the horses to their starting position so they would be ready to pull up the next stacker load. Occasionally, the horses didn't want to obey my voice to "git up" (which is the command to go ahead), especially at the end of their walk forward, where they had to pull extra hard to raise the stacker in a slightly tipped back position so the hay would fall down on the haystack. Dad would then come down from the haystack and give the horses "a lecture" in his loud, stern voice so they would listen to me again.

The stacker consisted of two long wooden arms, with a platform attached at the end that held the hay that Bernie piled there with a frontend loader, which was driven by a team of horses. I remember many long, hot summer days (95F), helping out in the field during haying season.

During the winter months, when the hay supply in the barn loft had been used up, Dad would haul hay in from the haystacks out in the field for the cattle to eat in the barn.

GROWING GRAIN CROPS

Beginning in early-to-mid May, when the warm weather had arrived, Dad used a team of four horses to plow and disk the fields and then seed the crops of wheat, barley, and (sometimes) oats.

Usually by mid-to-late August, when the grain fields had ripened, Dad started the harvesting. Using four horses to pull the binder, he went round and round the field, cutting off the grain, which then slid off the side of the binder tied in bundles, called sheaves. (Later on, the tractor was used to pull the binder. I remember driving the tractor, while Bernie sat on the binder to trip the bundle carrier when four sheaves had been tied and were ready to be dropped onto the field.)

Dad would then stack six sheaves together in an upright position, making what we called a "stook." He continued walking all over the field until all the sheaves had been made into stooks so the grain could dry out completely. When Bernie and I were old enough to help, we "stooked" together. We each took a sheaf and then propped these two sheaves together in an upright position, then we added four more sheaves to complete the stook. It was a wonderful sight in the fall to see hundreds and hundreds of stooks standing smartly like soldiers on guard all over the fields!

When the stooks were dry, it was time to thresh the grain. The owner of the big threshing machine (pulled by a tractor) and his threshing crew of about six to eight neighbor men, each driving a team of horses pulling a hay wagon, would come to our farm to begin. The threshing machine was set up in the field. It was powered by a wide belt that was driven round and round by the tractor's drive pulley. The men drove their teams among the stooks, stopping as they went by, to pitchfork the bundled sheaves into the hay wagons until they had a full load. Then the men, two at a time, drove up beside the threshing machine (one on each side) and, with their pitchforks, unloaded the bundles, one at a time, onto the conveyor table that fed them into the threshing machine. The machine separated the grain from the straw – grain was discharged from one spout into the nearby granaries, and straw was shot out from another spout onto what became a huge straw pile.

The threshing boss and his crew usually threshed the crops for most of the families in the neighborhood. Some of the crew didn't always go home at night; instead, they slept in the hayloft overnight, eating all their meals at the "host" farm.

Women were kept extremely busy cooking for all the men when threshing was occurring at their farm. A breakfast of porridge, meat, eggs, fried potatoes, toast, coffee, etc. was served at the house at 6 o'clock in the morning, then a mid-morning lunch of meat and cheese sandwiches, cake, cookies, and coffee was brought out to the field to be eaten by the men. The crew returned to the house for the full noon meal, which usually consisted of fried chicken or roast beef, potatoes, gravy, vegetables, bread or rolls, pie, coffee, etc. In the middle of the afternoon, another hearty lunch was brought out to the field for the men to eat.

Everyone came back to the house at 6 o'clock in the evening for the big evening meal, which was much like the noon meal that had been served.

I remember waking up in Mom and Dad's bed when I was four years old, and listening through the curtain (that hung in the bedroom doorway) to the men talking as they ate breakfast in the other room. When I got older, I helped Mom prepare the meals at the house and take the lunches out to the field.

One fall day, Dad came home (after visiting with a neighbor) in the middle of the afternoon and told Mom that the threshing crew of about six to eight men was coming to thresh our crops earlier than expected – in fact, that very afternoon! They would be having supper at our house that very day. Oh, dear! Mom's supper was still running around on two legs in the barnyard. Somehow, she prepared a full supper meal, complete with fried chicken, by 6 o'clock that evening.

HAULING FIREWOOD

We used wood for cooking and for heating the house. Every winter, Dad chopped down trees, then hauled them on a horse-drawn sled and piled them some distance away from the house, where they would dry out for a year. The previous year's pile of logs, now dry, had to be cut up for firewood. A neighbor brought over his wood-cutting saw that was powered by the tractor's drive pulley, and, with the help of a few more neighbors, the entire pile of logs was sawed into chunks in one day. This was called a "wood-sawing bee." Dad would then help out with wood-sawing bees at the other neighbors' places; this way there were no labor costs for anyone.

The wood had to be chopped up for heating and cooking and for kindling, which was used to start the fires. When Bernie and I were old enough, it was our job to carry armloads of chopped wood into the house to fill the wood boxes. We chopped the wood ourselves, using an axe, when we were older.

School Days

OUR HOUSE AND farm buildings were built on the west quarter of the half section of land we had at home, which placed us in the Benjamin School District. (The east quarter was in the Symonds School District.)

Benjamin School was nearly four miles from our home. It was an old, one-room, rural school, built in 1907, with a small porch on the north end through which we entered the building. Five tall windows, built on the east side, provided daylight for the schoolroom. The school grounds, about two acres in size, were fenced in and still partially treed. An old-fashioned hand pump, for drawing drinking water, stood near the school. A big pile of chopped wood, used for heating the school during the cold fall-winter-spring months, was stacked a few feet away from the west backside of the school. (A shed was eventually built to house the chopped wood.) Two outhouses – one for girls, one for boys – were placed some distance away to the south of the school. A barn, able to hold about twelve horses, was built near the back of the school grounds; this is where the pupils who rode to school tied their horses during the day.

While we went to the Benjamin School, Irene Wingate, a young woman who lived nearby with her parents, was hired as janitor to clean the school and to build the fire when it was needed.

Bernie (age 7, almost age 8) and I (age 6, soon age 7) started school in early December 1942 when Mom was asked by the Benjamin School Board to teach for the remainder of the school term. They had been unable to hire a teacher that fall. Bernie and I had been "home schooled" up until that time, so when Mom began teaching, she placed both of us in grade two. After a couple of months, however, she moved us up to grade three to finish out the school year. (This put me two years ahead of my normal grade in school.)

A new teacher, Miss Ross, was hired to teach the next year. Bernie and I were in grade four when we attended our first "full" year of school in the fall of 1943. Dad and Mom had bought us each a horse so we could ride to school. Bernie's horse was called Bluebell. He was young, light dappled-gray in color, and a bit feisty. (I found him hard to handle.) My horse was called Babe. She was a few years older, reddish bay in color, and very gentle. Her right, hind foot turned a bit outward (club foot); however, this didn't cause her to limp when she walked or galloped.

Miss Ross taught school at Benjamin for two years. One afternoon, near the end of grade four, Miss Ross gave Bernie (age nine) and me (age eight) a sealed letter to take home that she had written to our mother. (Because Mom was also a teacher, they occasionally exchanged letters.) Bernie sat just ahead of me in a row of seats, and together we decided to open the letter and secretly read it right there at our desks. Oh! Oh! Miss Ross caught us! She immediately scolded us - the whole classroom heard what we had done. Now that we were exposed, we felt so *humiliated* and so *guilty*!! We were scared when we got home from school that day, as we shamefully confessed to Mom what we had done. (It was very obvious that the letter had been opened!) Fortunately, after Mom reprimanded us for our misdeed, she lovingly forgave us but said we should never do that again. Lesson learned: DO NOT open letters that are addressed to other people without first having their permission.

Another afternoon, during Miss Ross' second year of teaching, (I was still eight years old, but now in grade five), a party (was it for Halloween?) was held at the school, and many parents had come. Someone suggested that all the girls line up according to grade level at the front of the room to tell what they hoped to be when they grew up. Some of the girls said they hoped to be a nurse, others hoped to be a teacher, or work in a store, etc. Because I had never given this question any thought before, I was puzzled by what

I should say. So when it was my turn to tell what I hope to be when I grew up, I nervously blurted out the only thing I was familiar with – I said I wanted to be a farmer's wife! The parents all laughed, which made me feel so embarrassed by the "stupid" answer I had given. (After many, many years, however, I finally DID become a farmer's wife – look in the Epilogue chapter to read about it.)

In the fall of 1945, Mom taught at the old, one-room Potter Creek School, which was approximately four miles north of our farm. Mom had to teach because most of our crops in the field had been damaged by hail that summer. Bernie and I went to school with Mom - we were in grade six. Even though we had to make new friends at this school, we enjoyed our year there. Mom was the last teacher to teach at the Potter Creek School because the next year all the students rode the school bus into Rimbey to attend school there.

Bernie and I went back to Benjamin School to complete grade seven and eight. I was only 10 when I entered grade seven. This was the most challenging year for me academically because the subject matter that we studied was more difficult than what we had covered in grade six. Fortunately, at the end of the school year, I squeaked through and was passed on to grade eight. (During the rest of my school years, I found it easy to keep up with my studies.)

Not many students came to school when the

winter weather was extremely cold. During our last year at Benjamin, when Bernie and I were in grade eight, we rode to school until the temperature dipped down to -25F (-32C). When it was colder, we stayed home too. To keep warm, on those very cold days, the eight or nine of us (who showed up for school) pushed our desks around the tall, round stove that stood in the back corner of the room. We often brought pint jars of chocolate milk from home and placed them in the warm water in the reservoir at the top of stove so we would have something warm to drink at lunchtime.

The school day began at 9:00 a.m. and ended at 3:30 p.m. In mid-morning we had a fifteen-minute recess, at 12 o'clock we stopped for a one-hour lunch break, and then in the afternoon we had another fifteen-minute recess. During our free time, we played various games outside. Some of the games we played were: Pump Pump Pullaway, Anti-I-Over, Hide and Seek, Prisoners' Base, Run Sheep Run, Red Rover, softball, marbles, hopscotch. In the winter, the teacher sometimes gave us permission to skate on a nearby creek during the noon hour.

Our school also had a softball team, so many recesses were used for practice sessions. In the spring, the team and the teacher and the rest of the students would occasionally go to a neighboring school during the afternoon to play against that team. Benjamin School played against the Andrew School, and Potter Creek School played against the Midland School.

The annual Christmas concert, presented before the entire community, was one of the highlights of the school year. This was always held the night before our Christmas holidays began. We students eagerly looked forward to these concerts; however, it was a great deal of work for the teacher, who had to organize it all.

At the beginning of December, various skits, poems, and carols were assigned to different students to learn. Two weeks before the concert was to be held, practice sessions began in earnest, usually during the last hour of the school day. Some men in the community built a stage across the front of the classroom; steps were built at both ends to access the stage. Curtains, hung to hide what was going on behind, were ready to be pulled open and shut as needed by the different acts. A large Christmas tree, decorated by the students, stood on the floor at one side of the stage.

At the end of the concert, Santa Claus (who was one of the men in the community) came through the crowd of people and walked up to the Christmas tree to hand out the gifts that were piled underneath. Every child in the community was also given a special Christmas bag that was filled with candy and peanuts - and a Christmas orange!

The night of the Christmas concert seemed "magical" for us! Dad put bells on the horses that pulled the cutter. I still remember hearing the rhythmic *jingle-jingle* as the horses trotted down the road during the cold winter night to bring us to the school and back home again. We kept snug and warm in the sleigh; our knees were covered with blankets and our feet were tucked inside the straw piled on the cutter floor.

Other community social events were also held at the school, such as evening dances (some of the local men provided the music), whist card games, and bridal showers. As children, we enjoyed playing together outside in the dark during these events. Every family brought sandwiches, cookies, or cakes, to be served with coffee at the close of the evening.

When World War II ended in May 1945, two official men came to our Benjamin school to tell us that the war in Europe was finally over. We were given the afternoon off to celebrate the event. Several young men in our neighbouring communities had served in the war.

These are the teachers Bernie and I had in the two country schools:

Grade 2-3 - Mom
Grade 4 and 5 - Miss Ross
Grade 6 - Mom
Grade 7 - Mr. Ingraham
Grade 8 - Inez Johnson

Inez Johnson was a substitute teacher. Benjamin couldn't get a teacher that year, so she supervised the correspondence courses that we received from the

Alberta Department of Education. In May and June, we were assigned a new teacher who had just completed her year of Normal School (teacher training). I don't remember her name.

At the end of the school year, when Bernie and I finished grade seven and eight, the Benjamin School held a community potluck picnic at Gull Lake, which was approximately thirty miles to the east of us. We kids had a lot of fun splashing and playing in the warm lake water, sometimes riding in small boats near the shoreline if an adult went with us, building castles in the sand, etc. It was a wonderful ending to a long school year.

Our years of attending a one-room country school had now come to an end.

World War II

WORLD WAR II began in 1939, and Canada immediately joined England in fighting against Germany, Italy, and Japan. Because Dad was still a German citizen, the Royal Canadian Mounted Police (RCMP) confiscated Dad's 22 rifle. After the war ended in 1945, his rifle was returned to him. (Dad never did take out Canadian citizenship.)

Many items were rationed in Canada during the war years, e.g. sugar, tea, coffee, butter, bread, certain types of meats, women's stockings, gas, etc. Everyone in the family, including infants, was given a ration book, which was issued through the Post Office. The ration book held coupons for only a certain amount of different items that could be purchased each month. I only remember sugar being rationed because we had meat, bread, and butter on the farm, and the rest of the rationed items didn't affect me. Dad had a sweet tooth and would often use up his allotted amount of sugar before the end of the month. He would then dip into Bernie's and my allotted portions of sugar, much to our annoyance, until we were allowed to buy more when the new month rolled around.

Life changed after the war ended: the Depression years of the 1930s were over; the economy was improving, and people were becoming more prosperous; rural schools were being phased out; and students were being bussed into schools in nearby towns.

Mom and Dad bought their first radio in 1940, soon after the war started, so they could follow the latest war news. One evening, as dusk was closing in, a man from the Rimbey hardware store drove out to our farm to bring us the radio that we had just purchased. I was four at the time. I had never listened to a radio before, so I was at first very intrigued by the mysterious "talking" coming from the back seat of the car when there obviously was no one sitting there. (The radio was turned on!) Mom happened to mentioned to the man that my name was Iris, to which he then replied, "Irish, eh?" I was embarrassed when he didn't say my name correctly. I'm sure he was just joking, but at the time, the teasing comment went totally over my head.

Some of the half-hour radio programs that Bernie and I listened to were: *The Green Hornet, Superman, The Lone Ranger*, and *Fibber McGee and Molly*. (Every episode of *Fibber McGee and Molly* played the sound effects of the contents of McGee's over-stuffed closet tumbling out onto the floor when he opened the closet door.) Radio programs were wonderful because we could use our imagination to "see" what was happening! Mom enjoyed listening to *Ma Perkins, As the World Turns*, and others during the noon hour. These were 15-minute-long programs, sponsored by different types of soaps, e.g. Ivory (with the well-known slogan, "99 and 44/100% Pure"). Hence, the word "Soaps" came to mean these short noon hour programs.

Because the economy was now picking up, Mom and Dad were able to buy a new dark green, three-quarter-ton Fargo truck in the spring of 1946. I remember sitting inside the truck, when it was parked in front of our house, and soaking up the new "car smell" and marveling at the fact that we now had a vehicle that we could ride in!

Encounter with Native Indians

WHEN I WAS young, many families of Blackfoot or Cree Indians (both tribes lived in Alberta) still roamed the countryside on horseback, seeking employment.

One summer, when I was four years old, a large family group of native Indians, including children, came to live and work on our farm for a few weeks. Dad had recently had the trees cleared off a 14-acre parcel of land that lay adjacent to the back field on our home place. The Indians were hired to dig out the tree stumps and gather up the branches, roots, and rocks that were still scattered all over this newly cleared land, so that Dad could then break (plow) the virgin soil to get it ready for planting crops.

When the Indians arrived, they came through our barnyard on their horses and rode out to the field where they would be working. They set up their tee-pees at the edge of the field - here they lived while they stayed on our farm.

One day, Bernie and I accompanied Dad when he

went out to where the Indians were working. Because everything in their campground and their way of life seemed so strange to me, I hid behind Dad's legs while he talked with the men who spoke English. However, Bernie, was braver than I was. He lifted the entrance flap of a nearby tee-pee to see what it looked like inside, and we saw the face of a startled, little boy peeking out at us!

Another day, some of the Indian women rode into our barnyard and then walked up to our house to "speak" with Mom. They held up a length of cloth, which they had bought, and, via sign language, asked Mom to sew a dress to fit the little girl who was with them. Several days after Mom had finished the dress, we found a three-pound lard pail full of wild blueberries sitting on our back doorstep. The women were saying "thank you" for the sewing Mom had done!

After the Indians had finished working on our farm, Bernie and I scoured the area where they had camped, looking to see if they had left anything behind. The only things we found were a few bunches of colorful beads, which we took home with us to use later when we played together.

In the fall, many native Indian families gathered near the foothills of the Rocky Mountains in central Alberta to hold their annual sun dance ceremonies.

I am grateful that I had the opportunity to experience this encounter with the native Indians because their nomadic way of life would soon disappear.

Iris with Bobby 1942

Bernie, Dad, and Iris 1942

Mom on Fairy 1943

*Benjamin School, Iris and Bernie 2nd + 3rd in front,
Spring 1943*

Bernie with Ginger, Iris with Pinky 1944

Bernie with Bluebell, Iris with Babe 1946

Dad, Betty Anne, Iris pumphouse in background 1947

Iris with a new look, starting grade 9 in town 1948

Our enlarged house - old part on the right 1949

Original house attached to the new part 1949

Miscellaneous Notes

HERE ARE SOME additional memories that seem to call for a chapter of their own. They have been jotted down in random order.

I was born around seven o'clock in the morning on the farm. Dad delivered me because the doctor didn't arrive at the house in time.

When Bernie and I were young, we liked to eat "Zucker Ei" (translation: "sugar egg," pronounced "tsooker eye"). We would beat four or five raw eggs together in a large bowl with a hand-held egg beater until the mixture was light and fluffy, then we would add enough sugar to sweeten it. *Yum!*

One morning, while Mom and Dad were milking cows in the cow barn, Bernie and I (we were about age six and five respectively) decided to whip up some Zucker Ei to enjoy while our parents were out of the house. Something was wrong with our beating this time because we couldn't get the eggs to whip up. So we decided to pour the egg mixture outside on the grass far enough away from the house where it wouldn't be noticed that we had wasted several eggs. But as I came out the back door with the bowl, I tripped on the step, and the bowl with the egg mixture fell out of my hands and landed on top of a nearby rock and broke. Oh! Oh! The evidence of what we had done was there for Mom and Dad to see! And to top it off, I had broken one of Mom's good bowls!

I had my first taste of watermelon when Mom's oldest sister, Lydia, and her husband, Jappe, (from Minnesota) came to visit us one summer.

Our allowance started when we turned five years old. We were given a penny a day, which was paid to us at the end of each month. On my fifth birthday, I remember getting a small, red coin purse with 25 cents tucked inside, which I thought was quite a treasure.

When I was about four, and Mom and I were home alone, I asked her what a "picnic" was. She said, "I will *show* you what a picnic is." She put a small tablecloth inside a basket, along with a few small sandwiches, some cookies, some milk, and two napkins. Mom carried the basket, and we walked to the edge of the cow pasture north of the house. She spread the tablecloth out on the grass among the trees and then put the food and napkins on the tablecloth. We both sat down and ate our picnic fare! What fun!

By the time I was 10 years old, I had caught the mumps, chicken pox, and the German measles from the other students at school.

I started baking apple pies when I was 10 years old. (I still use this recipe today, although I no longer bake them in the heated oven of a wood-burning kitchen range like we had on the farm.)

Here is my apple pie recipe: peel four large baking apples, cut into thin slices, spread evenly in an unbaked pie shell, pour three-quarter cup of white sugar evenly over the sliced apples, place five or six dabs of butter around on the apple/sugar filling, then sprinkle a bit of cinnamon (to taste) over everything. Place a top crust that has a few slits cut into it (so steam can escape during baking) on the pie. Bake in a 425 degree preheated oven for 15 minutes, then turn the oven down to 375 degrees, bake another 30 minutes (or until the apples are done). Delicious served with vanilla ice cream.

When I was four or five, I was rocking quite vigorously in our wooden rocking chair in the living room – *back and forth, back and forth* – when suddenly I flipped completely over backwards and landed on the floor, with the rocking chair on top of me. Ouch!

One winter morning, we became alarmed when we heard fire flare up in the chimney in the wood-burning heater in the living room. Flames started spewing out the top of the chimney, and the wind was sending sparks flying onto the shingles. Dad and Bernie raced up onto the roof via ladders with pails of water, which they then poured down the chimney before the roof could catch on fire and burn the house down. Whew! Close call!

Speaking of fire, one day, Dad and Bernie were working at our quarter section of land that was one-and-a-half miles north of us. Somehow the big barn in that farmyard caught on fire. The flames were too big to extinguish and the wind was too strong. The barn and several attached sheds burned up. Fortunately, Dad and Bernie were able to keep the house, which stood some distance away, from burning up too. We never lived there. However, the house was once used during the fall to cook and serve meals to the threshing crew that was harvesting our crop on that quarter of land.

For a few years, we sold one quart of raw milk every day to the Porters, who rented the house on the farmland across the road from us. They had no cows. We left the milk on their side of the fence, and then they would walk the quarter mile through the woods to pick up the milk.

During the summer months, we often had at least one heavy rain that would last about three days. Our road had no gravel on it, so this heavy rain made our road almost impassable for a while.

Our living room floor had only boards on it. A small crack had developed between two boards in one place. One day when I was three or four years old, and before the crack had been repaired, I squeezed my hand into the crack to pick up a spoon that I had dropped through there. My fingers somehow got pinched together as I pulled my hand out of the crack, and I ended up losing my left "pinkie" fingernail.

When Bernie and I were in grade five, to make extra money, we ordered valentines through the Winnipeg Free Press (a national newspaper) and sold them to our school friends for 5 cents each, others were three for 10 cents. We then reimbursed the newspaper for our valentine purchase and kept the remainder as our profit. We also sold vegetable seeds in the springtime. We rode our horses around to the neighbours in our community and sold the seeds for 5 or 10 cents a package.

In the early spring, we enjoyed eating cooked "pigweed" as spinach, which tasted so good after not having eaten any fresh greens during the winter months. (Pigweed was a weed that grew in the pig pen; hence, the name.)

I was eight years old, when Mom allowed me to walk about one mile alone through our neighbour's woods to play with Sally Cummings, who was twelve years old. She was the girl that lived the nearest to our place.

During the Easter holidays, when I was 10, Bernie and I stayed several days at our Grandma Eritsland's place. Her youngest son (our Uncle Paul) lived with her and ran the farm. They had a telephone on a party line (which is described in the Epilogue) in their dining room; other people shared this line too. Because we didn't have a telephone at home, we were quite intrigued by this instrument. One day, the telephone rang someone else's ring number, so Grandma or Uncle Paul didn't answer it. However, Bernie and I decided to lift the receiver and quietly listen to the people talking with each other. Uncle Paul happened to come into the dining room and caught us listening on the telephone. Oh, oh! This was a "No-No" and Uncle Paul sternly reprimanded us. Lesson learned: DO NOT listen in on party lines (which today are almost obsolete).

Mom and Dad always bought a large box of macintosh apples so we could have one apple a day to eat.

Bernie and I never had a bicycle when we were growing up. Our farmstead was located in a valley with steep hills on both sides, so there wasn't much room for riding bicycles. Sometimes we rode our friends' bicycles at school.

A small bridge on the road was built over the creek that flowed through our pigpen. There was a rather deep pool of water at one end of the bridge. Here is where Bernie and I spent a lot of time playing during the summer holidays - we looked for frogs, tadpoles, bugs, different insects, etc.

Usually, the weather in January and February would be very cold for a number of weeks, so we always welcomed the warm "Chinook" weather that blew in across the Rocky Mountains from the Pacific Ocean and lasted for a week or two.

On the afternoon of Christmas Eve day, Dad took Bernie and me with him into the woods to cut down a spruce tree. We pulled this Christmas tree home through the deep snow, set it up in our small living room, and then decorated it together. We had no electricity, so real candles were clipped onto the spruce boughs to light up the tree. We only burned these candles on Christmas Eve and New Year's Eve when we were in the room.

Mom baked her traditional fruit cakes for Christmas in November.

Here are the words we called out when we wanted our animals to come:

For cows: "ca' boss, ca' boss"
For pigs: "pig, pig, pig"
For chickens: "chick, chick, chick, chick"
(We didn't have a call for the horses.)

I loved to read. Mom and Dad made a point of buying some of the children's classics for us to read at home, e.g. *Tom Sawyer, Huckleberry Finn, Heidi, The Secret Garden, The Prince and the Pauper, Black Beauty*, etc. The only access I had to other books was at the school library. I remember reading all the *Grimm's Fairy Tales* when I was in grade six at the Potter Creek School.

After we all had vehicles, our nearby uncles, aunts, and cousins would meet together in the summertime at Grandma's house to enjoy a potluck picnic lunch and then stay for lots of visiting afterward. We all loved these times!

I wore my hair in two long pigtails while I was going to the one-room country school. Because my hair was so long and thick, Mom found this style the easiest way to keep my hair from becoming tangled. By the time I was 10 years old, I braided my own hair in the morning. I was glad that I was allowed to cut my hair short and curl it when I entered grade nine.

When our nearby neighbours, the Cummings', built a new barn, they held a huge barn dance and invited everyone in the community to come. I was about nine years old at the time. I had lots of fun playing in the barnyard in the dark with all the other young children who came with their parents.

There was no television when I was growing up. All the drama stories were read on the radio, with all the appropriate sound effects to make the drama come alive in our imaginations.

I felt intimidated by the children who lived in town. They had friends who lived nearby, whereas our friends all lived some distance away. I didn't realize, until I was older, that the town children envied those who loved on the farms!

A Terrible Shooting Incident

THE LEAD-UP TO this terrible incident in 1948 actually began several years earlier.

Sometime in late August or early September in 1944, Dad and Bernie were walking in the field on our home place when suddenly they heard a shot and a bullet whizzed past them. They looked around and saw a man with a rifle standing nearby at the edge of the field. Dad hollered, "What do you think you are doing?" The man pointed and said, "Deer! Deer!" giving the impression that he was shooting at a deer. Then he quickly disappeared into the trees. Dad didn't recognize the man. *Why was this man hunting on our private land?*

The next year (early September 1945), Dad went out in the morning to cut grain with the horses and binder in the back field on our home place. Before cutting, he left his noon lunch of sandwiches inside one of the nearby granaries. But when he stopped to eat his lunch at noon, he discovered that someone had eaten it! Mom had just started teaching that fall at the Potter Creek School (approximately four miles north of us) because much of our crop had been badly damaged by a hailstorm that summer. Bernie and I went to school with Mom, so the rest of us weren't home that day. Mom and Dad became rather alarmed after this incident, knowing someone was skulking around on our farm.

Another more threatening incident happened the following year (early September 1946) while Mom was in the Rimbey hospital after giving birth to Betty Anne. Dad was walking behind a team of four horses, driving them to our north quarter, one-and-one-half miles away, to start cutting grain with the binder. (He had left the binder there after cutting the day before.) Suddenly, one of the horses shied and looked to the east into the bush beside the road. Even though Dad couldn't see clearly, looking toward the sun, he saw a man with a gun standing in the trees just inside the fence beside the road allowance. Dad asked the man what he was doing, and the man called out "Wait" (or something to that effect), then aimed his gun at Dad. Dad immediately shouted to the horses, "GIT UP," but, as they started, he felt a tug on his shoulder and knew he had been hit. He stopped at Neumeiers, neighbors who lived about one-quarter mile farther down the road, and tied up the horses there. Dad begged a gun from Neumeirs and then went back to the spot where the shooting had occurred, but he found nothing. Dad walked home with the horses, unharnessed them, and then drove to the Rimbey hospital to get his wound taken care of. Then he went to see Mom to tell her that a man had just tried to kill him.

After speaking with Mom, Dad reported this attempted murder to the police. Dad told the police they should check the hotel registers in Rimbey to see if anyone from out of town had stayed there in early September during the last several years when all these suspicious events were taking place. The police, however, said no one would be foolish enough to register under his own name if he intended to kill someone, so the hotel registers were never checked.

Mom and Dad decided not to mention this shooting incident to Bernie and me at the time, so that we wouldn't become afraid. They told us later after Mom was home from the hospital with Betty Anne.

For protection, Dad now purchased a full-grown, female German shepherd dog, named Queenie, who could be quit vicious, to accompany him as he worked around the farm. Mom hung bed sheets over the windows at night during this time of year so no one could see inside when the lamps were lit.

Nothing happened the following year, (in early September 1947). However, Mom and Dad were on high alert because of what had happened over the last several years during this same time period. Was the stalker sick? Was he dead? Was this nightmare finally over?

It was a late spring that next year (1948) because Dad hadn't yet completed all his seeding in the fields. On June 2, Dad was planning to finish the seeding (using a drill, pulled by a team of four horses) on our north quarter. It was now late, around eight o'clock in the evening, and Bernie and I were waiting on the road outside our driveway, hoping to see Dad coming home. We finally saw him drive the horses with the drill down the first hill south of our mailbox and then drive down into a dip in the road, where we could no longer see him. That was when we heard a loud shot! Then we saw our dog, Bobby, running down the next hill, but we didn't see Dad with the horses and Queenie, the other dog, coming behind him. Something was wrong!

We hurried into the house to tell Mom what had happened. She and Bernie jumped into the truck and quickly drove up the road to see what had happened. (I stayed home with Betty Anne, who was not quite two years old.) Mom and Bernie found Dad kneeling on the road with blood all over his head. He had been hit in the head by shotgun pellets. But he was still conscious! The shooter could have fired another shotgun blast to finish the job right then, but he must have left immediately after shooting Dad. The horses were standing caught in the bushes in the east ditch; the fastest horse on the team had been hitched up closest to the west side of the road, from where the shot was fired, and reacted the quickest, turning the team toward the ditch.

Bernie helped Mom get Dad inside the truck cab, and then Mom quickly drove off to take Dad to the hospital in Rimbey. Bernie unhooked the horses and drove them home into the barn and unharnessed them. Bernie and I waited in the house (without any lights on), with a gun across Bernie's knees, for Mom to come home. Our emotions were running high. We were stunned and scared for Dad's life and recovery.

Mom came home about 11 o'clock that night. She told us that Dad said (as they were driving to the hospital) he couldn't see out of his right eye and thought he had lost the sight in it. The doctor in Rimbey sent Dad by ambulance the next day to the University Hospital in Edmonton where he needed surgery to remove his damaged eye.

Mom now began to make plans to go to Edmonton. She phoned Mrs. Ellis to ask if she could stay at her place while she was visiting Dad in the hospital. (Mom had lived with the Ellis family in her late teens while she completed her high school in Edmonton.) Mom then phoned her brother, Paul Eritsland, who lived with Grandma on their farm near Leslieville (30 miles away, near Rocky Mountain House) to ask him to come and stay with Bernie and me while she was away in Edmonton. Mom also phoned her sister, Ida Lowe, who lived with her family on a farm near Blackfalds (30 miles away in another direction, near Lacombe) to ask if Betty Anne could stay there while she was away. All of Mom's siblings agreed not to tell

Grandma at this time about Dad's shooting "accident" because they knew Grandma would become very worried and upset about what had happened.

The next day, Mom rode the bus to Edmonton to be with Dad at the hospital. Later that afternoon, Uncle Paul drove out to our farm to stay with Bernie and me. He then drove both of us and Betty Anne to Aunt Ida's so we could leave Betty Anne there. Aunt Ida's 14-year-old daughter, Betty, came back with us to the farm to help with the work and to keep us company.

Dad stayed in the Edmonton hospital for 10 days. He came home with a glass eye inserted in his right eye socket. After he arrived back home (in mid-June), several of our neighbours came and helped finish seeding the crops at our home place. (Dad ended up with several shotgun pellets in his scalp, and, occasionally, over the years, one would work itself out.)

News of Dad's shooting was reported on CKDA, Alberta's major radio station. Now the police investigation quickly got underway. When the police investigated the scene where the shooting had taken place, they found a blind made of branches and leaves (which the shooter hid behind) set up in the trees just inside the neighbour's fence on the west side of the road where Dad would be driving by on his way home from work that evening. It was obvious that the perpetrator had been following Dad's current work schedule. Ironically, Dad had broken something on the drill around noon that day and had walked home (unsuspectingly past the blind!) to get a part to fix it. Mom had then driven him in the truck back to the field to finish his seeding.

Up until this time, the police had always thought it was a disgruntled neighbour or relative who had done the previous shootings. But now the police DID check the Rimbey hotel registers and asked Dad (at the hospital) if he recognized any of the names listed there. The name "Pete Rokowski" stood out immediately! He was the Polish immigrant who had worked for Dad for about a month in early 1939. (I don't remember Pete Rokowski staying with us.) Pete had helped Dad build our big horse barn. Incidentally, at the time, he had written his name on the inside of the barn door. I had occasionally glanced over at his name when we were milking in the barn.

Now the police had a possible suspect they needed to find. They learned by checking recent bus passenger lists that Pete Rokowski had arrived in Rimbey before the shooting and then had left immediately afterward for Edmonton, where he had purchased a ticket for Prince George, British Columbia. Pete was apprehended by the police at the Edmonton bus station. At first, Pete denied knowing Dad or having ever been to our farm. (Dad had told the police they would find Pete's signature written on our barn door.) The police came out to our farm and confirmed that it was indeed the same signature that Pete Rokowski had used when he signed the hotel register. Later it turned out that the only thing Pete could write in English was his name. That's why he didn't register under a false name. (He had always signed in as Pete Rokowski during those previous years when he came back to Rimbey.)

Pete eventually confessed to the shooting and to his previous years of stalking Dad, with the intent to kill him. Pete turned out to be mentally disturbed. He said he wanted to kill Dad because he thought Dad had tried to poison him when he was working for us. Pete said that, one night after supper, Dad had poured the remaining contents from Pete's glass of milk into the cat's food dish. The next morning, the cat was found dead. In his mixed-up mind, Pete assumed that the milk had been poisoned, and, therefore, he deduced that Dad had tried to poison him!

Pete Rokowki was charged with attempted murder and held in jail until his trial, which took place in Rimbey later that year. Dad, Mom, and Bernie attended Pete's trial; I stayed home with Betty Anne. Pete was found guilty and was committed to the Ponoka Mental Hospital, where he died a few years later of cancer.

Later it was revealed that after working for Dad, Pete ended up with a job in Saskatchewan. His yearly holidays were always during late August to early September. This is why he was able to return to Rimbey during that time of year to reconnoitre our farm. Did Pete change jobs after 1946, which resulted in his having a different holiday time? (In 1948, Pete came in early June, instead of early September.) Apparently Pete realized he was a poor shot with a rifle because this time he brought a shotgun, which he had traded his rifle for in a gun shop in Edmonton. He wanted to make sure he would hit his target this time! Even so, the shotgun mostly missed Dad - had the full blast hit Dad, he would have been killed.

The reason Dad didn't recognize Pete Rokowski when Dad confronted him in the field in the 1944 "Deer! Deer!" incident or when Dad saw him briefly in 1946 by the roadside (when the rifle shot glanced off his shoulder) was because Pete had lost a great deal of weight during the years since he had worked for us.

Bernie (age 13) and I (age 12) were both in grade eight that year. We didn't return to school for the rest of the school term (which ended June 30) after Dad's shooting incident because we had to do the chores at home while he was in the hospital and while he was recuperating at home. We had to milk eight or nine cows by hand, feed the pigs, grind chop for the animals, pump water for the cattle, feed the chickens, gather the eggs, chop wood to fill the kitchen wood box, haul water to the house, etc.

Later that summer, while Dad was still recuperating, Mom cut a door through the wall that separated our old house from the much larger newly finished addition that our parents had started building in 1943. Now our house was BIG!

Epilogue

OUR YEARS OF attending a one-room schoolhouse had come to an end. That fall (1948), Bernie and I caught the school bus nearly three miles north of our home farm and rode to Rimbey to take grade nine. Then in the fall of 1949, we both began our high school years (grades 10-12) at Concordia Lutheran College in Edmonton, graduating in 1952.

Thank God that Dad survived his tragic shooting incident, otherwise, (1) my siblings, Linda and Mark, would never have been born, (2) my life would have taken a very different path because Bernie and I would not have been sent to Edmonton for our high school years, (3) I would never have met my first husband, Rudy Nast, my high school boyfriend, who became a Lutheran pastor, (4) I would not have had the children that I was blessed with, (5) nor would I have met my present husband, Marlin Goebel, who was a member of the Lutheran Church in Hillman, Michigan, when my first husband ministered there.

In 1953, Mom and Dad were able to have the rural party telephone line installed, which was three-quarters of a mile from our house. Dad and Bernie had to cut down the trees along the side of our road so that the telephone poles could be put up. The telephone hung on our kitchen wall immediately to the right of the washstand. The telephone had a mouthpiece (to speak into) in the center, a handheld receiver (to hear the speaker) hung on the left side, and a hand crank (for "ringing" the numbers) was placed on the right side. People on rural party lines had telephone "rings" (sounds) that were made up of long and short rings (e.g. two longs and one short or one long and one short and one long, etc.). To call a neighbor on the party line, the hand crank had to be turned for a "long" ring, stopped, then turned again for another "long" ring or turned briefly for a "short" ring, stopped again, and so on, depending on what type of rings that person had. When we heard our ring, we picked up the receiver and answered the telephone. To call someone on another party line or long distance, we had to go through the operator, who then placed the call for us.

Electricity was brought to our farm shortly after the telephone was installed. The power was first put in the barn (for the milking machine), in the pump house (to pump water), and in the kitchen. Soon the rest of the house was wired for electricity.

Dad didn't have enough money to move back to

Germany to live because (1) soon after he arrived in Canada the Great Depression years began, (2) he married and started a family, and (3) then World War II began. Sadly, he never saw his mother again.

In 1960, Dad's oldest sister, Elisabeth (Tante Lisa), and her daughter, Barbara, came to Canada for a visit – this was the first time he saw any of his family since he had left Germany in 1929. In 1965, Dad was financially able to return to Germany for a three-month stay to see his homeland once again and to visit with the rest of his family (two sisters, a brother-in-law, and a niece). This visit worked out well for Dad because his daughter, Betty Anne, was living and studying in Germany at the time. He died in 1968.

In her later years, Mom taught school for a few years in Rimbey. After Dad died, she continued living on the farm until Mark, the youngest, finished high school. After that, she lived in Rimbey for a number of years before relocating to Red Deer, where she lived in an apartment that was built alongside a combined assisted living complex and nursing home. Later, because of failing health, she moved into the nursing home. She died in 1994.

My brothers, Bernie and Mark, inherited the farm, but neither of them farmed there; instead, they sold the land. The one quarter (one-and-one-half miles north of us) was bought by the Trautman family, and the three quarters at home were bought by the Heilemann family. No one ever lived on our farm again. The Heilemanns bulldozed all the farmyard buildings and fences, except for the big barn Dad had built in 1953 and the two car garages. (Our farmhouse had burned to the ground several years before while it stood vacant.) A large herd of cattle is pastured on this farmland now, and crops are planted in the fields.

Rudy Nast and I were married on June 10, 1956; he still had two years of seminary training to complete – the first year he served a vicarage (apprenticeship) in Abbotsford, British Columbia, then he returned to the seminary in Springfield, Illinois, for his final year. After graduating in 1958, Rudy served the following congregations: a triple-parish in Mannville, Vegreville, and Bruce, Alberta (1958-1962); Tooele, Utah (1962-1967); Great Bend, North Dakota (1967-1968); Hillman, Michigan (1968-1970); and Victoria, British Columbia (1971-1972).

Rudy and I had twelve children: Heather, Barbara, Alana, Timothy, Kimary, James, John, Darren, Laurel, Shauna, Ryan, and Coral. (Their birthdates and places of birth are listed in the Chronology chapter.)

Unfortunately, Rudy struggled with re-occurring mental health issues throughout our marriage and eventually had to give up the ministry. He then worked for many years in the garage service industry. Due to continuing ill health, he departed from our family in 1984, and then divorced me in 1986.

After Rudy left, I worked for two years in home-care; I had to arrange day care for my four youngest children when they were out of school. In 1987, I attended a community college for 12 months, taking computer and business administration courses. After my training, I was immediately hired by the British Columbia government, where I worked for nine years. I retired on January 31, 1997, and moved to a townhouse complex in Sooke, which is a bedroom community of Victoria.

On August 6, 2011, I married Marlin Goebel, who was now a widower. The previous December, we had renewed our forty-year-old friendship. Marlin is a retired high school science teacher, and still raises certified organic grain-fed angus beef cattle on a large farm. He has four children (Kurt, born September 18, 1961; Kathy, born November 22, 1962; Keith, born July 25, 1967, Kory, born November 28, 1971).

Together, Marlin and I presently have 79 people in our family - this includes children & their spouses, grandchildren & their spouses, and great-grandchildren! We have been richly blessed.

"All things work together for good to them that love God." (Romans 8:28)

Chronology

1854, August 22 - Baron Bernhard von Tettenborn (my German grandfather) was born.

1864, November 7 – Lars Eritsland (my Norwegian grandfather) was born.

1867, April 30 – Anna Marie Alsvag Eritsland (my Norwegian grandmother) was born.

1879, November 1 – Elisabeth Muller von Tettenborn (my German grandmother) was born.

1988-1989 – My Norwegian grandmother and grandfather respectively immigrated to the USA through Ellis Island, in Upper New York Bay.

1889, May 25 – my Norwegian grandparents were married in St. Paul, Minnesota.

1904, February 18 – my German grandparents were married.

1906, July 6 - Baron Bernhard von Tettenborn (Dad) was born in Tilleda, Prussia, Germany.

1907, June 19 - Alma Eritsland von Tettenborn (Mom) was born in Nassau, Minnesota.

1909 – Mom moved with her parents and siblings to Eugene, Oregon.

1911, July 26 – my German grandfather died in Tilleda, Prussia, Germany.

1916 – Mom moved with her parents and four youngest siblings to a farm in Central Alberta, Canada.

1929, April 22 – Dad entered Canada at Pier 21 in Halifax, Nova Scotia.

1930, June 2 – my Norwegian grandfather died in Leslieville, Alberta.

1932, October 29 – Rudy Nast was born in Grand Prairie, Alberta.

1933, October 13 - Mom and Dad were married in Leslieville, Alberta.

1934, December 18 – my brother, Bernhard (Bernie), was born on the farm.

1936, February 21 - I was born on the farm.

1936, April 21 – Marlin Goebel was born in Alpena, Michigan.

1939 - World War II began.

1943, December - Bernie and I started school in Benjamin School; Mom was the teacher.

1944, late summer/early fall – Dad's nightmarish shooting incident began.

1945 - World War II ended; Mom began teaching in the fall at Potter Creek School; Bernie and I went with her to this school; during harvest time, Dad's lunch in the field granary mysteriously disappeared.

1946, September 6 - my sister, Betty Anne, was born in the Rimbey hospital; Dad was shot in the shoulder.

1948, June 2 - Dad had the shooting incident where he lost his right eye; the perpetrator was caught and later that year was sentenced to an insane asylum; in September, Bernie and I began riding the school bus to take grade nine in Rimbey; that fall, Dad bought a second-hand tractor, which greatly eased his farming operations.

 1949, September - Bernie and I started high school (grades 10-12) at Concordia College, a Lutheran high school and pre-seminary college in Edmonton.

1950, December 22 - my sister, Linda, was born at the Rimbey hospital.

1952, June - Bernie and I graduated from high school; that summer I got my driver's license, which cost one dollar - I was never asked if I could drive! (I had been driving in our fields since I was 12 years old); that fall I enrolled at the University of Alberta in Edmonton in the one-year teacher training program.

1953, January 15 – my brother, Mark, was born in the Rimbey hospital; in May and June, after I completing my teacher training, I taught grades 5-8 at the Hoadley one-room rural school; in September, I taught grade 1 at the Bluffton school for one year – I was 17 years old when I started teaching; the Baby Boomers (children born after World War II ended), had just started school, and education systems everywhere were desperate for teachers to teach this huge influx of new students.

1954, July and August - I attended summer school at River Forrest, a Lutheran college in Chicago, Illinois;

in September, I taught grades 1-4 for two years at Concordia Lutheran Parochial School, a two-room school, in Springfield, Illinois.

1955, June 9 – my German grandmother died in Minden, Germany; she often wrote letters to Bernie and me (in the old German script); we never met her.

1956, June 10 - I married Rudy Nast in Rimbey, Alberta; we moved to Abbotsford, British Columbia, where my husband served his year of vicarage in the Lutheran Church.

1957, June 15 – daughter Heather was born in Abbotsford, British Columbia; that September, we returned to Springfield, Illinois, to complete Rudy's final year of seminary training.

1958, June – Rudy graduated into the Lutheran ministry; he was assigned to serve a triple parish in north-central Alberta, Canada.

1958, December 6 – daughter Barbara was born in Mannville, Alberta.

1960 – Dad's sister Elisabeth (Tante Lisa) and her daughter Barbara flew from Germany to Canada to visit us for a month; Barbara stayed another two months in Edmonton to be mentored by a few doctors (she was a medical student at the time).

1961, January 27, daughter Alana was born in Vegreville, Alberta.

1962, February 6 – son Timothy was born in Vegreville, Alberta.

1962, June – moved to Tooele, Utah, to serve the Lutheran church there.

1962, December 4 – daughter Kimary was born in Tooele, Utah.

1963, December 3 – my Norwegian grandmother died in Alhambra, Alberta. (Both of my Norwegian grandparents never returned to their homeland; they each had one sibling living in America, but they never saw anyone else in their families again.)

1964, June 29 – twin sons, James and John, were born 11 weeks premature in Tooele, Utah; praise God, they were both baptized before they died a few hours after birth.

1964, December - I toured the Mexican border town of Tijuana when we visited with friends in Chula Vista, California, during the Christmas holidays.

1966, October 16 – son Darren was born in Tooele, Utah.

1967, February – moved to Great Bend, North Dakota, to serve the Lutheran church there.

1968, May – moved to Hillman, Michigan, to serve the Lutheran church there.

1968, November 4 – Dad died of a sudden heart attack out in the field.

1970, May – moved to Tawas City, Michigan, where our children attended the Lutheran parochial school.

1971, July 31 –moved back to Canada because we were Canadian citizens; arrived in Victoria, British Columbia (on Vancouver Island on the Pacific Coast).

1975, July 26 – daughter Laurel was born in Victoria, British Columbia.

1976, September 2 – daughter Shauna was born in Victoria, British Columbia.

1978, August 3 – son Ryan was born in Victoria, British Columbia.

1980, October 29 – daughter Coral was born in Victoria, British Columbia.

1984, August - Rudy left our family; he soon began divorce proceedings; I was now a single mother, left to raise our four youngest children by myself; in December, I began working fulltime as a homecare worker.

1986, September – Rudy's divorce from me was finalized.

1987, January – I attend 12 months of computer and business administration college classes in Victoria, British Columbia.

1988, January – I started working for the British Columbia government, three months with the Government Agents Office, the remainder of the time with the Ministry of Agriculture.

1990, June – I flew to Europe with Kimary and her two boys, who were four years old and 8 months old; in Germany we visited Dad's oldest sister, Elisabeth (Lisa), and another cousin, Erika, then travelled by train to Venice, Italy (we stayed two days), returned via Switzerland and Germany to the Netherlands, where Kimary was scheduled to give a talk in Amsterdam; we were gone two weeks; Alana and another family looked after my four youngest children in Victoria while I was away.

1994, August 5 – Mom died in Red Deer, Alberta, after suffering several years from Alzheimer's disease.

1997, January 31 – I retired after working for the British Columbia government for nine years; then I moved to Sooke, the most southwestern town in all of Canada, along the Pacific Ocean.

1999, July 2 – Rudy Nast, my first husband, died of lung cancer.

2000, July and August – our cousin Barbara, from Germany, flew to Canada for a lengthy visit with Bernie (Gladys) in Alberta, Betty Anne (Ian) in Ontario, Linda in Vancouver, and me in Victoria.

2003, July 11-14 – a large family reunion was held in Alberta for the descendants of our Norwegian grandparents; over 260 relatives attended, coming from all over the USA and Canada; several of our second cousins from Norway also attended.

2007, July 31 – my oldest daughter, Heather, died in Minneapolis, Minnesota, after a nine-year struggle with breast cancer.

2008, October – I flew from Vancouver, British Columbia, with my two sisters and a nurse friend to Beijing, China; we joined a tour group that travelled throughout China and Tibet for 25 days; we visited Tiananmen Square, the Forbidden City, the Great Wall of China, the city of Xian where thousands of buried terracotta soldiers were recently unearthed in a nearby field, the panda breeding facility in Chengdu, flew to Lhasa, Tibet (the rooftop of the world) where we climbed to the top of the famous Potala Palace, took a three-day river cruise down the Yangtze River and passed through the nearly completed Three Gorges Dam, then flew out of Shanghai to return to Vancouver; to get to all these different tourist sites, we took seven different flights within China.

2010, August – I travelled for four weeks in the Middle East with my daughter Kimary and her husband Khaled as their guest; I first flew to Qatar to visit with them there (they are foreign workers in that country); from there we all flew to Amman (in Jordan) and Ramallah in the West Bank (in Palestine/Israel) to visit with Khaled's family, who live there; we travelled by car to visit Jerusalem, Bethlehem, Jericho, the Dead Sea, the Sea of Galilee, Cana, Nazareth, the Mediterranean Sea, Haifa, and Akka. Never in my lifetime did I envision that I would visit these places in the Holy Land!

2011, August 6 – I married Marlin Goebel in Port Orchard, Washington; we live on our farm in Hillman, Michigan, raising certified organic black angus beef cattle.

2013, January 29 - my brother, Mark, passed away in Red Deer, Alberta; he suffered a heart attack the day after his 60th birthday and died 13 days later; Marlin and I attended his gravesite memorial service in August.

2014 – God-willing, two more great-grandchildren will be joining our family.

PRAISE GOD FOR ALL HIS BLESSINGS!

"Oh, give thanks unto the Lord, for He is good! For His mercy endureth forever." (Psalm 136:1)